THE KIDS' LIBRARY OF MARTIAL ARTS™

TAE KWON DO

Pamela Randall

The Rosen Publishing Group's
PowerKids Press™
New York

Published in 1999 by The Rosen Publishing Group, Inc.
29 East 21st Street, New York, NY 10010

First Edition

Book Design: Danielle Primiceri

Photo Illustrations: pp. 7, 8, 11, 15, 16, 18, 19, 20, 22 by Seth Dinnerman; p. 4 by Ira Fox.

Randall, Pamela.
    Tae kwon do / by Pamela Randall.
        p.   cm. — (The kids' library of martial arts)
    Includes index.
    Summary: Introduces the history, basic moves, and terminology of this martial art.
    ISBN 0-8239-5233-9
    1. Tae kwon do—Juvenile literature. [1. Tae kwon do.] I. Title. II. Series: Randall, Pamela.
    The kids' library of martial arts.
  GV1114.9.R36 1998
  796.815'3—dc21
                                                    97-49271
                                                      CIP
                                                        AC

Manufactured in the United States of America

Contents

Evan Starts Tae Kwon Do School

Evan is going to take classes in tae kwon do. There are several other ways to spell the name of this **martial art** (MAR-shul ART), including taekwondo and tai kwon do, but they all mean the same thing. The name is Korean. In English, it means "kick-strike-art" or "foot-fist-art."

On his way into the tae kwon do school, Evan meets Christine. Christine has been taking lessons for three months. "You're really going to like tae kwan do," Christine tells him.

◀ *Even young kids can learn tae kwon do!*

Why Study Tae Kwon Do?

Like other martial arts, tae kwon do is a form of **self-defense** (SELF-dih-FENS). It is a lot like karate. Kids like Christine and Evan who study tae kwon do will learn how to protect themselves. Tae kwon do teaches people more than just protection. They also learn about **self-discipline** (SELF-DIH-sih-plin) and building **confidence** (KON-fih-dens).

Christine is studying tae kwon do to stay fit and healthy. Evan is taking tae kwon do so he won't feel afraid of the bullies at school.

Learning a martial art, such as tae kwon do, can help you feel more confident about yourself. ▶

High Standards

Self-discipline is a big part of tae kwon do. Students learn **self-control** (SELF-kun-TROL). For example, Evan will learn from his tae kwon do teacher that it's important to do things like finishing his chores and homework and practicing his tae kwon do moves before he goes out to play.

Some tae kwon do teachers will not advance their students unless the students do their chores and homework. And this is true even if the kids are doing very well in tae kwon do class.

Tae kwon do instructors teach their students more than moves. Students are taught how to use self-discipline to improve themselves in many different ways.

Tough Teachers

Tae kwon do **instructors** (in-STRUK-turz) expect their students to be **dedicated** (DEH-dih-kay-ted) to learning tae kwon do. Instructors make sure their students know how important it is to practice at home and to attend classes regularly.

Instructors also expect their students to be disciplined. Students know they can't get away with bad behavior in class. They won't be able to move up to the next rank, or skill level, until they show the instructor that they are serious about tae kwon do.

In order to advance, students need to show their instructor ▶ that they have practiced their moves and know them well.

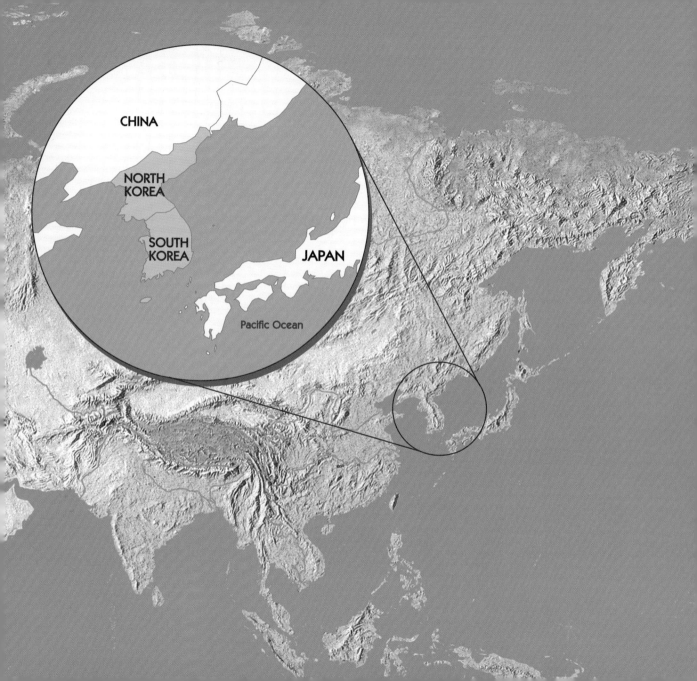

CHINA

NORTH
KOREA

SOUTH
KOREA

JAPAN

Pacific Ocean

Where Tae Kwon Do Got Its Start

Tae kwon do got its start in the 1600s. It was taught to young **noblemen** (NOH-bul-mun) in an area that's now part of Korea. These young men were trained in defense so they could protect their kingdoms. This training was a little like the basic training taught to modern-day soldiers in many countries today, such as the United States.

A form of those moves from so long ago is the tae kwon do that is taught today.

Korea is part of East Asia. All martial arts were created in East Asia.

Something for Everyone

Tae kwon do is very popular throughout the world. While some people like Evan take tae kwon do lessons for self-defense or self-discipline, there are other reasons to study this martial art. Like Christine, some people may want to use it as a form of exercise for a healthy body. Other people take tae kwon do because they love sports but don't have time to play on a team. With tae kwon do, you don't need a team to practice. It's something you can do whenever you want.

Not all kids are the same, so their reasons for studying tae kwon do may all be different. ▶

It Takes Practice

Tae kwon do moves are simple. But students in class must repeat these moves over and over. This way, the moves will be as natural and familiar to them as walking.

Tae kwon do is taught in a **dojang** (DOH-jang). *Dojang* is a Korean word for training hall. The teacher, also known as a master, is called a **sabumnim** (sah-BOOM-neem).

During class, kids stretch, practice moves, and **spar** (SPAR) with other students. They also learn how to **meditate** (MEH-dih-tayt). This helps them relax and focus on their moves.

◀ *Things such as meditating and stretching help students stay calm and relaxed during their lessons.*

Stances

The way you stand when doing tae kwon do is very important. If you spar with your **opponent** (uh-POH-nent) from the wrong **stance** (STANS), you could lose your balance and fall. Because of this, tae kwon do has fifteen basic stances. Advanced students learn even more than that!

18

The back stance is used often in tae kwon do. While in a back stance, you can kick. You can also give a straight fist punch. There are two steps involved in doing a back stance. Both steps are shown on these pages.

No Forks or Spoons

In tae kwon do, the outside edge of the foot is called the knife. It is used for side kicks and for kicks to certain parts of the body. Evan and Christine will learn to aim for an opponent's knee, neck, head, and **abdomen** (AB-duh-min).

The hand is sometimes called a knife too. Depending on how you use your hand, it might also be called a spear or a hammer. The knife hand position is what most people picture in their minds when they think of a karate chop.

◀ *In tae kwon do, size doesn't matter as much as skill.*

Christine and Evan Meditate

Christine and Evan meditate before class. Meditation helps them **concentrate** (KON-sen-trayt). Then they won't get **distracted** (dih-STRAK-ted) when they spar.

Evan and Christine will learn to erase thoughts from their minds. Christine may concentrate on her breathing. Evan may think of a short sound, like "Ahh." And he will think only of that while he meditates.

Since they started tae kwon do, Christine is healthier and stronger than she's ever been. And Evan is a lot more confident. He isn't scared of bullies anymore.

Glossary

abdomen (AB-duh-min) The lower belly.

concentrate (KON-sen-trayt) To focus your thoughts and attention on one thing.

confidence (KON-fih-dens) A firm belief in yourself and your abilities.

dedicate (DEH-dih-kayt) To devote yourself to something.

dojang (DOH-jang) The Korean word for training hall.

distract (dih-STRAKT) To have your attention drawn away.

instructor (in-STRUK-tur) A person who teaches someone how to do something.

martial art (MAR-shul ART) Any of the arts of self-defense or fighting that is practiced as sport.

meditate (MEH-dih-tayt) To relax by sitting quietly and emptying your mind of thoughts.

nobleman (NOH-bul-man) A member of royalty or other high-ranking person in a kingdom.

opponent (uh-POH-nent) A person who is on the other side in a fight.

sabumnim (sah-BOOM-neem) The Korean word for master.

self-control (SELF-kun-TROL) To control your actions or feelings.

self-defense (SELF-dih-FENS) To protect yourself against an attack.

self-discipline (SELF-DIH-sih-plin) The ability to make yourself do the things you should.

spar (SPAR) To have a practice fight.

stance (STANS) A position you stand in when fighting.

Index